For Maudlin Muses & Pretentious Poets

Jamie Mudle

BookLeaf Publishing
India | USA | UK

Jamie Mudle

Presentation by *BookLeaf Publishing*

Web: www.bookleafpub.com

E-mail: info@bookleafpub.com

ISBN: 978-93-5744-938-0

First edition 2022

DEDICATION

For Aleksandra.

ACKNOWLEDGEMENT

With thanks to:

Bookleaf for putting this out there and running the challenge that led to this book, my editor Alex without whom it would have been a mess, and my hype man Prijay for the wonderfully inflated biography.

PREFACE

The basic idea behind this book is to put something out into the world for better or worse. I like the idea that a poem can invoke, in very few lines, a feeling that one couldn't reasonably describe, not with a picture, nor even with a thousand words.

Though should your poem be a thousand words long, it will either be full of feeling or feeling full.

That feeling is entirely subjective depending on the reader, but maybe one of them might stir something up in you.

Maybe the inspiration to do better. I'm confident you can!

Primrose Eve

Through my open window creeping
Warm summer air came stealing
Bringing sounds of farmhands reaping
Their fields of wheat, the daylight fleeting
The children's laughter was defeating

On that Primrose Eve

I sat draining tumbler, into slumber
While the endless warmth of summer
Brought endless gnats with vicious bites
Oh, how I cursed the dwindling lights

On that summer's eve

With cruellest winter over the horizon
Malice filled shadows did I lay my eyes on
Bringing with them death's embrace
Draining colour from my face

On that autumn's eve

And as the clock hands struck midnight
A stranger's darkness stole the light

So through my open window creeping
Came death’s dark grip, coldly reaping
My mortal soul, my life repeating
The children's laughter was redeeming

On that winter’s eve

Alone

There's a cloud over the hill
And the road curves round the bend
The air is getting still
As the journey nears its end

The maelstrom, now is growing
When I pull up to the house
Angry, now the wind is blowing
Trees waltz, as if by Strauss

I've been trying hard to reach you
But there's no answer on the phone
Of where you've gone, I've got no clue
But I'm sure you are alone

Do you hear me at the front door?
I've been trying to get in
The silence chills me to my core
And my head begins to spin

Success, at last, the back door pops
Flies forward with the gale
I look around, and my heart stops
What's that liquid in the pail?

I’ve been trying hard to reach you
But there’s no answer on the phone
Of where you’ve gone, I’ve got no clue
But I’m sure you are alone

In panic now, I climb the stair
One first, then two, then three
I shout your name into the air
Yet you do not answer me

All rooms but one are unsealed
All rooms but one are clear
All rooms but one revealed
All rooms but one grow fear

I’ve been trying hard to reach you
But there’s no answer on the phone
Of where you’ve gone, I’ve got no clue
But I’m sure you are alone
The howling now is come inside
The final door is barred
This madness I cannot abide
Fork lighting strikes the yard

And in time with the thunder
I crash straight through the door
With barely time to wonder
What you’re doing on the floor

I’ve been trying hard to reach you
But there’s no answer on the phone
Now I know where you’ve got to
And I’m sure you aren’t alone

A Ghost In The Hotel

There's a ghost inside the hotel
Everybody tells me so
By the window you can hear them well
But who it is, I do not know

The bellhop thinks it's his ex-wife
Who died three years ago
But I saw her starting a new life
Leaving footprints in the snow

The chef thinks it's an ancient ghost
From many years now past
A soldier killed while at his post
Sadly not the last

The manager thinks suicide
For he's seen it all before
He's wrong as well, though many tried
And it happens more and more

The maid thinks it's a lonely hound
One that the dead can see

She’s right, of course, as I have found
The hound lives here with me

Upon My Brow

On a brisk cold morning
I'll wake up yawning
Make plans for what I'll do
They don't seem so unique now
They won't be done with you

Things are fine, well I suppose
But in my heart the feeling grows
I'll buy a coffee, take a seat
Some memories I can't allow
For in those there's defeat

A walk in the park
Never was so dark
As when it's done alone
This yearning pit I must avow
As it hardens into stone

Cold is the pillow as I awake
And reach across for old times' sake
In time, I'm told, the feeling fades
And I can make it through somehow
Until then, I draw the shades
With tears upon my brow

A Good Life

A good life is hard to define
Once we're allowed to grow
Like sea upon a shoreline

There is no stop sign
So we just go
Follow the preset line

To the temple shrine
Inside the city grotto
Enough to eat, but not to dine

A place to sleep, the stars to shine
For someone else to know
That we cannot consign

Ourselves to fate, this grand design
Where fickle winds will blow
Turn gentle soul into malign

Our separate threads now align
Conspire now to show
When offered fear one must decline
A good life? Courage must define

Influence

Sometimes I think I'd like to leave
See the world from the road
Where "What's for dinner?" is the only load
On my mind, a brief reprieve

Then at once, I can believe
That maybe my pace should be slowed
That life is no more than borrowed
And a new path we can weave

I'd buy a dog and then a van
Or maybe walk forever
Take pictures, write words, make video streams

So you could follow my new plan
Leave your soul light as a feather
You can pursue your dreams

The truth is I'm so full of shit
I'm bursting at the seams

Creation

Am I the same as he
Or she or they who made these works?
Could such art stem still from me?
Am I where creation lurks?

Could I sculpt this stone?
Carve this wood?
Bring life to this alone?
And if I could, does it mean I should?

Or is it just my arrogance
That brings me now to think?
That I could bring from word or tense
An artistic missing link?

And once it's brought
Into existence
I'll question if I ought
Or if it's justified resistance

And so it always seems to be
That once it's written, then it's free

For The Sea

Many miles and all uphill
To reach the lookout point
It saps all strength and takes my will
To get here weakened every joint

At times I wished the trip was shorter
That I'd packed a little better
In the end, I'd used my water
And ended up no wetter

As now I stand and look upon
Tumultuous tempest far below
I feel the breath of Poseidon
As his rage breaks in the shallow

I can hear the boom from my perch
It resonates with thunder
Here is a very different church
Though no less filled with wonder

Whose power moves these gentle waves
With such force to shake the earth?
Is it the same that damns or saves?
And just what is that worth?

When I stare out across the sea
Who is it staring back at me?

Choices (Haiku)

Choices, right or wrong
Decided by intention
Ruled by reflection

Define My Love

Define my love, passion, desire
The kind that all great works require
How it can be for simple things
Like dogs and cats and diamond rings

Perhaps there's more complexity
In the way the light came through the tree
When you told me of your hopes and dreams
Or the hours spent repairing seams
Of threadbare teddy bears, charity shop purchase
Laid out upon our kitchen surface

In a house we said was built with love
Unshakeable shelter for our hearts above
We placed our feelings on the wall
In pictures, keepsakes large and small

Around these objects, love can reside
But true love's the memories contained inside
Success and failure, highs and lows
The way our story ebbs and flows
The cross-eyed, giant, stuffed giraffe
That never failed to make you laugh

Passion said to define true love
Is not all that there is thereof
More underrated, with rarer mention
Is the undercurrent of intention

Of happiness that flows inside
Hearts' beachside view of the rolling tide
However felt, love can be chronic
Romantic, passionate, perhaps platonic
It takes root in hearts and spreads through veins
Some days it waxes, some it wanes

But never truly leaves completely
Hides in the background, waits discreetly
'Til at the perfect soulful moment
Bringing forth joy or mournful torment

Joy when you feel the perfect mixture
Of contentment, warmth, a snapshot picture
A memory from well-spent youth
Deciphering the simple truth
That a life with love's a bitter pill
But a life without is emptier still

Sunshine Sonnet

Warmth in sunlight's golden rays
Spread from one heart to mine
A million other summer days
Tarnish not the shine

Of when we spend one moment more
In conversation with each other
Out loud in public by the shore
Or hidden undercover

And when you're gone, there's nothing left
But to sit and pass the time
With heart and hearth and home bereft
While the mantel clock doth chime

Indeed I cannot covet more
Than to be with you, whom I adore

Beat In The City

There's something in the air tonight
Beneath the neon signs
A feeling it will be alright
If we read between the lines

Every stop along the way
To a place we've never been
We move in time, the notes that play
From an unheard band unseen

And anything can happen
While we walk the cobbled street
Our steps provide the tappin'
Of the city's new heartbeat

Maybe I'd even kiss you
Maybe you'll kiss me back
Or we'll kiss people totally new
Or no one at all and never know the lack

On the next street, there is magic
Food that's too good to eat
Or maybe something tragic
But no less easy to defeat

And anything can happen
While we walk the cobbled street
Our steps provide the tappin'
Of the city's new heartbeat

So when it's nearly closing time
And we're heading for the door
We'll tell ourselves it's not for me
To wish for something more

We'll join the growing exodus
Of people heading for the train
And if it's packed, we'll take the bus
Or stumble through the rain

And anything can happen
While we walk the cobbled street
Our footsteps stop the tappin'
As two heartbeats skip one beat

Cold Pillow

Quiet, in the mind
A soft breeze through the window
A few thoughts put to paper lined
The cold side of the pillow

Memorable scents upon the street
The sound of life around
A mild lungful of summer heat
While you laze upon the ground

Walking by the old oak tree
The flowers by the lake
Stop and pick a blackberry
Fall asleep, perchance to wake

Fine alone, in pleasant weather
It was always better, done together

In Wine, Is There Truth?

In vino veritas, in wine there is truth
Nevermore has Latin been more uncouth
What truth is there in a glass-eyed stare?
In showing all comers your underwear?

How honest should I feel when I'm leaning
Against the traffic light pole in a pose so demeaning?
What hero am I stumbling down roads in this frock
While my keys fumble vainly in every lock?

It's a lie when I shout after every shot
"That's it for me and I'm out; that's my lot!"
Hide all the bollards and signs when I pass
Lest I steal traffic cones to replace my wine glass

And if I tell you, I love you, and you're my best mate
By the morning I'll call you a bloody ingrate

I won't remember your name even tattooed on my face
Which it very well could be; there's a great tattoo place

Worse even still than drunk and too glad
Are the moments of being too drunk and too sad
Is it true then that I will be dying alone?
Not even a salesman to call on the phone?

So you see now that there's as much truth in this wine
As there is a good beach in Lichtenstein

Gone Walking

A scent born on a gentle breeze
Blows softly by the tree
Long moments spent where time can freeze
As we go walking, you and me

London's green and pleasant space
Stretches outwards over the horizon
A morning dewdrop on my face
More beauty than I've laid my eyes on

Into our hands and then our pouch
Do the ripe blackberries rest
You have never been much of a slouch
When it comes to seeing the very best

Atop the hill, I stare out over a backdrop framed by you
In all the years I've been here, you've been missing, don't you see?
And now I know within my heart how much this love is true
As we go walking, hand in hand, just you, my dear, and me

An Equal Share

I remember picking from the tree
Some fruit for you and some for me
Over time this became
A habit for us, more a game

See who can gather the most
Before the shadow hits the post
Before we have to head to our homes
To read more academic tomes

If our pockets are full with berry and date
Then can we be forgiven for turning up late?
Could we hope to beat the sun?
No time to walk, it's time to run!

Cross the river and jump the root
A foot wrong now a mud-stained boot
But long grass will leave it clearer
Although the evening's drawing nearer

I reach the edge before you, I've won this race
But in collecting fruit you're still first place
You see, you took the safer route
While in my haste, I lost my fruit!

And as we walk the long way back
Behind the lake, on disused track
We laugh at this misfortune
The time passed quick, we'll be home soon

Down the road is where we part
And here is where I see your heart
A smile in the eyes and with an honest laugh
You look at me and split the haul in half

So now we both have fruit to spare
As we turn for home with an equal share

Hope Springs (Haiku)

Warm feelings will come
Unbidden for me today
Contentment springs hope

Pendragons Quest

Fork lightning cracked sky as our heroes left
port,
Dark clouds o'er the horizon, bailing out is for
nought,
"To shipwreck bay, we'll sail, grab some
chickens today"
"I suppose we might as well, as we'll end up
there anyway"

Wind cracks against the rope and ropes constrict
upon the mast,
"This storm is damn inhuman; there's no way it
can last!"
And suddenly, with a deafening SNAP! the
planks rip away,
"It appears without some swift repairs we'll not
make shipwreck bay"

So grab the wood, the bailing bucket, make sure
those holes you mend,
Else you might find your final rest in a sinking
watery end,
Intrepidly, our heroes work, to secure their
sinking ship

And through their diligence and speed, these problems' bud, they nip

The journey on to shipwreck bay is rife with cheer and laughter,
The banjo plucks, and drums do ring well into the hereafter,
To be heard by one Arthur Pendragon, ghost hunter of renown,
Who fancies that he hears two folks, now fit to wear his crown

It should be mentioned at this point that this is not the same Pendragon,
Instead of lifting knights of old, he can barely lift a flagon
No round tables, horses, swords or stones exist within this sordid tail
And as our brave adventurers arrive, they quickly curl up their sail

And spy the chickens that they seek, one white and one that's black
No sooner have they landed when they come under attack
From skeletons with empty holes where once there were two eyes
Dispatching these quite quickly, they find a satchel of supplies

Gunpowder, wood and food is found within the tortured wrecks,
But hardly worth the continued risking of their necks
The smarter of the two pipes up, "There's something over there!"
"A ship, I think, so large that any treasure must be rare"

Inside the captain's chamber of the beached and broken ship,
Scattered books and ransacked timbers sea slicked enough to slip
And a painting hung behind an altar freshly lit
The painting reads, "Arthur Pendragon, ghost hunter, pirate, wit"

A book disturbed by searching hands, the painting now has stirred,
The ghost of A. Pendragon to this world has now been lured,
"Hello, oh fine adventurers, I finally can see
You must be mighty pirates, almost as much as me!"

"My life cut short by devil's curse, my story is much shorter
I freed souls trapped by evil, gave adversaries no quarter

Until the day I picked a fight with a dragon that was ashen,
A hundred years I've spent now trapped for the ardour of my passion"

"I ask you now to help me, to grant me my release,
Take my lantern and my journal, and soon this curse will cease
I had three souls to save before I ended up this way,
And if we find and free them all, my pain will surely end this day"

Our heroes, while more usually swayed by the lure of gold,
Decided the adventure would be worth the story told,
So, picking up the lantern and the journal on the table,
They headed back unto their ship to continue 'long this fable

"Don't forget the chickens first!" one of our characters did cry,
And so, they journeyed homeward for a dram or two of rye,
A kraken did pursue them as they headed back to shore,

But with a deftly fired shot, well, the kraken was no more

With other quests now squared away the journal they did read,
Only to find that shipwreck bay was where the path did lead,
So off they sailed again, with music fast behind their backs
And the lantern of Pendragon stashed safely in their sacks

"Eastwards of shipwreck bay is now our destination"
"Look over there! A ghostly ship, I have the eeriest sensation"
"Looks like a battle's being fought, let's sail on up and see"
"Maybe hang back? I just don't know; it looks dangerous to me"

They sail behind the shadows of battles fought before,
And arrive upon a shipwreck close to old forgotten shore,
"I see the gleaming skull down there among the broken timber"
"I'll swim down and grab it; thankfully, I'm pretty limber"

And so, our heroes dive among the wreck of ancient ships
But something deep within the water lays in wait and licks its lips
A shark as dark as midnight and tired of hiding in the hull
Approaches our adventurers just as they find the skull!

One hero spies it looming out and sizing up its marks,
"Probably a bad time to say this, but I'm terrified of SHARKS!"
And so, our brave, strong hero, gallantly he swims away
Leaving his friend behind so she can take the role of prey

"I understand you're scared, but I've got the bloody skull,
If you could just maybe shoot it? Before it turns me all rag doll"
But the shark is out of harpoon range, and our hero cannot see
"I do not want to worry you, but the shark is eating me!"

The skull is dropped, the other hero swims safely to the boat

An argument ensues about who's next to be the goat
"You've got a lovely rifle; why don't you shoot the shark?"
"You know I cannot use it, for I never hit my mark!"

"So I'll dive in and grab the skull it as I know where it lays,
And you can shoot the shark with your pistol if it strays"
"I just don't think I'll hit it..." our adventurer starts to say
But it's pointless as the other is already on her way

The shark has circled back by now, gracefully does it glide
A shot rings out from on the deck, and in shock, it turns to hide
"I've got the skull again! Now help me back onto the deck
Quickly, as the shark is back, and it's eyeing up my neck!"

She tries to swim back to the ship, but the shark is much too quick,
The blood upon the water is like Satan's own oil slick

Fear cast aside, the other jumps straight into danger rife
To try and save the skull and hopefully still save her life

Nobody can be seen throughout the murky blue
But the skull is floating nicely, and the shark has circled too
He grabs the skull with both his hands and turns quickly towards the shore
But a bite across the leg reminds him what he's rushing for

The shark comes back for seconds to enact its evil plot
It seems two heroes now lay dead when from the darkness comes a shot
"I killed the shark; I shot it!" Says our heroine with a shout
"It thought that it had got me! Doesn't pay to count me out"

On the beach, the skull is given to the ghost of A. Pendragon
And our heroes settle down, find a beach to hoist their flag on
Driving the ghostly sword straight through the centre of the skull,

From the sparks that fly out of this blow, this sword is never dull

A ghostly female figure now stands proud among the shore
And tells a story of betrayal, of misery and more
She trusted a man who ran away. Who can trust someone who steals?
"A man who runs away from danger? I'm sure I don't know how she feels"

Her spirit free, she gladly tells what she knows of where he went
Of the cowardly thief who met his end when his running days were spent
"Somewhere there is a group of islands, a volcano fire show
It's here this coward went, though where exactly I don't know"

Once more, our heroes venture out to find the next lost soul
Stopping quickly to grab a bit of shark to fry upon the coal

Without an idea of where exactly the next ghost could be found
Our crew takes no time to rest upon the safety of the ground

They check the fated journal, glowing wicked with green fire
And see two pages have been added, their words equally dire

"Fletcher's Rest is the place where the next skull resides
To get there you must cross more perilous tides"

"There seems to be a volcano on this drawing, and I think I know the place
I'll set a mark upon the map; we should sail there with increased pace!"
So while one of them sails, the other consults the haunted books
Searching for clues, more like detectives than mere hard seafaring crooks

And halfway 'cross the sea, they dodge a heavier storm
While below their feet, surges a far more ominous form
These waters must have monsters, as forests have bracken
For out of the waves lunges another kraken!

Looking up from his book, our hero now runs
To the front of the ship and its powerful guns
Aiming with the harpoon, Thrice he fires a shot

Two find their target, and one sadly does not

The kraken breaks free, is surprised that this
snack
Has the weapons aboard to mount such a vicious
attack
Slinking away far back under the waves
It waits for more minor morsels in these watery
graves

In short order, our heroes and their miraculous
ship
Arrive at an island and so take a dip
In the water, to head out over to the magma
soaked ground
But no sign of their prize is around to be found

Jumping back on the ship and consulting the
map
Another such target falls into their lap
An island quite similar, just a few miles away
Travelling there would take the rest of the day

But consulting the map, our learned hero has
spied
Their destination, misidentified
"Fletcher's Rest, it's here clear as day
It's now Fletcher's Folly Fletcher's folly, but this
must be the way"

While studying drawings of this new destination
It's noticed it bears a rather striking relation
To the very same island, they had sailed to at first
Ease is not natural, for this quest has been cursed

With a quick change of direction, they speed to the task
Flaming clouds of hot ash make a warm, choking mask
And the great balls of fire that shoot through the sky
Come so close to the ship as to kiss it goodbye

Deftly dodging the rocks and escaping the ash
They arrive at the scene of the next ghost ship's crash
Scramble onto an island, and they find the skull buried
Dig it up, hold it tight, and to their ally, it's ferried

While Pendragon is talking and freeing this ghost
Giant craters of steam open up on the coast
Like the island is breaking apart at the edges
The hot burst of steam tosses both over hedges

This steam does not touch the two ghosts on the shore
Information that our heroes wish they'd been given before
The Dragon of ash that Pendragon did fight
Slew this miserable captain and sailed into the night

But the ghost knew just where this new ship had fled
Marked its place in the journal in ink, dripping red
A quick stop for supplies at the nearest outpost
As our heroes consult the big book of ghost

To their surprise, the next goal is not far
The next island across holds the promised sandbar
The ship barely makes it ten metres away
When another eruption blocks out the day

This one is closer still, than the previous three
And a rock made of fire breaks the mast into tree
Four holes in the hull and the ship nearly flips
As our heroes are covered in ash and wood chips

Scramble quickly, my friends, and repair what you can

Lest you too join the others who came here with no plan
The final hole plugged as the water did rise
Nearly all the way past our heroes' clear eyes

The mast now repaired, they carry onto the mark
As the air all around becomes chillingly dark
But out in the distance can be easily seen
A giant brigantine, shrouded in green

"We should follow that ship to its final rest
But avoiding the rocks would also be best"
So they follow the markers and sail to the end
To cleanse Pendragon's curse and put his soul on the mend

There's a hole in the ground and a chest that they take,
But they begin to feel that this must all be a fake
There's nowhere to go, no skull to be found
Just an ominous grinding and a laughing sound

Skeletal shapes shuffle out of the mist
Some are moon bleached, others sun-kissed
With sword and gun, our heroes fight them off
Bone dust in the air brings on choking and cough

"Turn the lantern over there" one has the idea
That this terrible ornament may make it all clear
As the green light appears and bathes onto the walls
The whole thing does shudder, and the edifice falls

Revealing behind a coffin of stone
Filled to the brim with a giant of bone
The skull is just there, so they grab it and run
Straight into the barrel of a skeletal gun

The captain of the last ship, not a lost or trapped soul
But a creature of evil with only one goal
To defend this cavern from all who would dare
To defile its darkness with essence so fair

In one final fight, the two heroes with swords
Guns out of ammo against dread pirate lords
They slash and they hack until bones are laid bare
And the deadly bone captain faces his nightmare

They return him to dust and stumble outside
To give this coffin bound skull to the soul who had died
Pendragon is excited to have the last soul in hand

As he plants his ethereal feet deep into the sand

He runs his sword 'cross the top, as he's done twice before
When the island does shake with a deafening roar
A skull in the sky as large and red as the sun
Laughs as it asks, "did you think you had won?"

"I'm the most vicious pirate these islands had seen
Sealed up tight in a coffin for crimes too obscene
Locked away with a guard of my crew's undead souls
All undone by child pirates merely playing at roles"

"I suppose I should thank you for breaking this curse
But leaving you breathing would surely be worse
Now live in this world, which I'll burn with my fun"
And Pendragon sinks to the ground "My god, what have we done?"

Silence abounds as our heroes take to their ship
It'll take more than a grog to erase this damned trip
As they sail through the night and the sky, it does blacken
Deep beneath the waves surges another kraken

Goodbye From Me

Carbon forms send salutation
Through rocket-powered aviation
To leave some sign on lunar soil
Of how far we've come for all our toil

A snapshot of our world inside
Rests now and long past when we've died
And if by chance you do not know
Earth's ancient history now years ago

This hard drive should be quite the link
Twixt what we know and what you think
And if by chance we still exist
Through a miracle or cosmic twist

Then this should be quite the find
Something to expand the mind
Showing just what came before
That we were capable of more

In here that hope thrives and survives
It's the meaning of a million lives
All taken as a single snapshot
And labelled clear "forget-me-not"

We were once Earth and may still be
But if we're not, goodbye from me

This is the only piece in the book technically published elsewhere, as a copy of this poem resides as part of a lunar time capsule created by u/Valphon on the Reddit forums.

What's Next?

What’s next to go?
Be torn asunder?
The seeds we sow?
Our sense of wonder?

What’s next up on the chopping block?
Our right to live and learn?
What sense is there in taking stock
Of everything they steal and burn?

What’s next in line for kindling?
Our hopes, desires, dreams?
While you’re at work, they’re swindling
The very stitches from your seams

What’s next up for brutal cuts?
I’m not sure there’s much left
As service after service shuts
Leaving our country bereft

What’s next to turn this all around?
Bring those who graft to task
Lest corruption carry on unbound
And we’ll all be soon to ask

What's next?
What's next?
What's next?

The Last Rhyme

This last work is encoded for a little interactive exercise! It's a simple substitution cypher so for this, I'll start you off so T=A and the rest of the alphabet follows after. There should be a line after each, well, line so there's somewhere to fill in your answers.

It's entirely possible you may end up with something completely different in doing this but hopefully, it's at the very least slightly more entertaining!

Tgw ghp px kxtva max ybgte phkd

Ihxf mpxgmr hgx

Uxabgw mabl vhwx, whxl fxtgbgz enkd

Vhnvaxw bg t lihm hy yng

By rhn'ox wxvbiaxkxw xoxkr ebgx

Rhn ftr ux phgwxkbgz par

B'ox vahlxg mh tllbzg

Vhwxw phkwl tl t lir

Mknma bl B tiikxvbtmx

Rhnk inkvatlx hy mabl uhhd

By rhn wbwg'm, lvtgwtehnl kxikhutmx

Maxg B'f zetw rhn mhhd t ehhd

Lh ftgr matgdl yhk rhnk lniihkm

Yhk max fnlbgzl hy t ehhg

B'ee dxxi mabl hgx fxkvbyneer lahkm

Unm B dghp B'ee ux utvd lhhg.

www.ingramcontent.com/pod-product-compliance
Lightning Source LLC
Chambersburg PA
CBHW051737130826
49812CB00033B/899
* 9 7 8 9 3 5 7 4 4 9 3 8 0 *